William
Boeing

Community
BUILDERS

William · Boeing

Builder of Planes

by
Sharlene
and Ted
Nelson

Children's Press®
A Division of Grolier Publishing
New York / London / Hong Kong / Sydney
Danbury, Connecticut

Photo Credits

Reading Consultant
Linda Cornwell, Learning Resource Consultant
Indiana Department of Education

Visit Children's Press on the Internet at:
http://publishing.grolier.com

Library of Congress Cataloging-in-Publication Data

Nelson, Sharlene P.
   William Boeing : builder of planes / by Sharlene and Ted Nelson.
     p. cm. — (Community builders)
   Includes bibliographical references and index.
   Summary: A biography of William Boeing, a pioneer in the development of aviation and the founder of the Boeing Company, which started out building military and transport airplanes and now builds most of the world's passenger jet aircraft.
   ISBN: 0-516-20973-6
   1. Boeing, William Edward, 1881–1956—Juvenile literature. 2. Boeing Company—Juvenile literature. 3. Aircraft industry—United States—History—Juvenile literature. [1. Boeing, William Edward, 1881–1956. 2. Boeing Company. 3. Aircraft industry—History.] I. Nelson, Ted W. II. Title. III. Series.
TL540.B622W45 1999
338.7'6291'092—dc21
[b]   98-27760
                                                       CIP
                                                         AC

Contents

William Boeing

Chapter ONE

Planes for the World

Have you watched a jet plane flying high in the sky? Have you greeted friends or relatives at the airport when they arrived on a jet plane? Maybe you have flown on a jet plane.

Chances are the planes you have seen or flown on were built by The Boeing Company of Seattle,

Washington. The largest of these planes can carry four hundred passengers. They fly 7 miles (11 kilometers) above the earth at speeds of 600 miles (966 km) per hour.

Today, The Boeing Company builds most of the world's passenger jet aircraft. Its planes are flown by nearly six hundred different airline companies in sixty countries. Boeing planes link communities around the world with only hours of flight.

The Boeing Company was started by William E. Boeing. His first plane carried one passenger. It flew a few thousand feet in the air at 70 miles (113 km) per hour.

William Edward Boeing was born in Detroit, Michigan, on October 1, 1881. His father Wilheim was a German immigrant who became a wealthy mine and forestland owner. William's mother Marie was from Austria. As a young boy, William attended private schools in Switzerland and the United States. At Yale University, he studied engineering to learn how things are made and how they work.

When William attended this air show in 1910, airplanes were called "flying machines."

William Boeing came to believe that much could be accomplished with careful thought and hard work. In 1903, a year before graduation, he left Yale and went to Washington State. He was twenty-two years old.

With his family's wealth, William bought forestland in Washington. He was interested in boat-building and bought a small shipyard in Seattle. In 1910, he watched planes flying at an air show. William decided that he wanted to fly.

The World's First Plane

The year 1903 marked the world's first airplane flight. The plane was built by brothers Orville and Wilbur Wright in their bicycle shop in Dayton, Ohio. They shipped the plane to North Carolina where the sand dunes at Kitty Hawk would provide a soft landing.

On December 17, Orville and Wilbur made several flights at Kitty Hawk. The longest flight lasted fifty-nine seconds and covered 852 feet (260 meters).

Orville Wright flies the first airplane as his brother Wilbur runs alongside.

Boeing Builds His First Plane

Villiam Boeing met a young navy officer named Conrad Westervelt. Conrad knew how to design and build boats, and William asked for his help with a yacht he was building. They also shared an interest in planes and became good friends.

One day in 1914, a pilot brought his two-winged pontoon plane to a lake near Seattle. (A pontoon plane is equipped with floats, called pontoons, that enable it to take off from and land on the water.)

10

**Many early planes were equipped with pontoons,
instead of wheels, for water takeoffs and landings.**

First William, then Conrad, took rides in the plane.
The pilot and his passenger wore goggles and sat on
the front edge of the lower wing.

Wooden Boats and Wooden Planes

Boats and planes were a lot alike in the early days of flight. Like small boats, planes were framed with wood. Many planes took off from and landed on water because there were few airfields. Instead of wheels, planes had wooden pontoons built like small boats.

The engine roared, and the plane hurtled across the water. As the plane became airborne, William could see the city below and snowcapped mountains in the distance. William knew that people were meant to fly.

William's first flight was on this plane in 1914.

After more flights, William said to Conrad, "There isn't much to that machine. I think we could build a better one." Conrad agreed, and they began to design a plane. They called it the *B & W* from the initials of their last names.

Conrad Westervelt left Seattle before the design was completed. William hired a Chinese engineer named Tsu Wong. Tsu finished the design, then skilled boatbuilders used strips of wood to frame the body, its two wings, and the tail. Women sewed linen cloth over the wood frames. A small engine was mounted in the front.

In this photograph, taken about 1916, women sew cloth over the plane's wood frames. The cloth was then shellacked to make it strong.

The *B & W* was the first Boeing airplane.

On June 15, 1916, the *B & W* rested in the water on its two pontoons. William had learned to fly, and he climbed into the open cockpit. As a few of his employees watched anxiously, the plane skimmed the water then rose into the air. William's flight was successful and marked the company's beginning. The next month he formed Pacific Aero Products Company. Later, the name was changed to the Boeing Airplane Company.

Chapter THREE

Flying Farther

After a second *B & W* was completed, William Boeing and his twenty-one employees went to work on another plane. It was the Model C. William let engineer Tsu Wong try out new ideas for the plane, even though the pilot, Herb Munter, thought they wouldn't work.

On November 23, 1916, Herb flew the first Model C. As he thought, the tail was not properly designed. The plane nearly spiraled into the water before Herb could regain control.

16

How Planes Fly

A plane's propeller creates thrust that moves the plane forward. Thrust overcomes drag (the resistance of the air). With speed, the wings are lifted, just as your hand is lifted when you tilt it outside the window of a moving car. The wing's lift overcomes the downward pull of gravity. To control the plane's flight, the pilot uses the engine's throttle and moves parts of the wing and the tail.

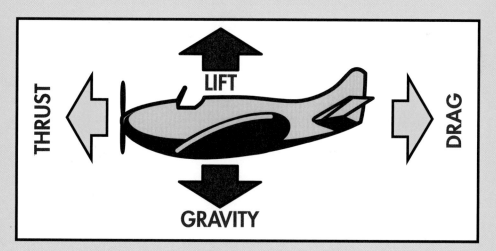

This diagram shows how planes fly.

**William Boeing stands on a pontoon
to help ready a Model C for flight.**

Tsu Wong began improving the plane's design with growing urgency. World War I (1914–18) had begun in Europe, and people thought that the United States would soon be in the war. William knew the military would need planes.

On April 8, 1917, the United States declared war against Germany. The next day Herb Munter successfully flew the redesigned Model C. William Boeing arranged for test flights with the U.S. Navy.

Then, Tsu Wong left the company to return to China. William hired Claire Egtvedt and Phil Johnson. Both had studied engineering at the University of Washington. These two men would play important roles in the company's future.

Claire Egtvedt

Phil Johnson

Soldiers guarded Boeing's plant, later called the "Red Barn," when the company was building military planes.

The Model C was flown in tests for the navy in competition with planes made by other companies. The navy liked the Model C and ordered fifty as trainers for navy pilots. When one of the planes was delivered, a navy inspector found a frayed control cable. The cable was repaired, but poor workmanship distressed William. He wrote, "I for one would close up shop rather than send out work of this kind."

The company also received an order to build fifty military planes designed by another company. Nearly four hundred people were working at Boeing plants. The main plant, a big, wooden building later called the "Red Barn," stood on a riverbank near Seattle.

Seattle, Washington

Seattle is built on hills above the waters of Puget Sound. Founded in 1851, it was named for Chief Sealth who was a leader of two American-Indian tribes. In 1914, one skyscraper stood in the city. Today, Seattle has many skyscrapers and is home to about 500,000 people.

Seattle

Chapter FOUR

"A Splendid Future"

World War I ended in November 1918. William Boeing knew there would be no orders for military planes for a while. The U.S. Post Office needed planes to transport mail, but it would use planes left over from the war.

Still, William told his employees, "I look for a splendid future in peacetime." Then he added that, for a time, "It will be a hard struggle." Because there were no orders for new planes, the company's employees were reduced to eighty. They built boats and furniture.

When there were no orders for planes, William kept some of his employees at work building boats.

Claire Egtvedt, however, worked on plans for a flying boat called the B-1. The plane's body, like a giant pontoon, would rest in the water before flight. Its engine, mounted below the top wing, would provide enough power to carry a pilot, two passengers, and a cargo of mail. William hoped the flying boats would bring passenger and airmail service to the northwest, as well as buyers for new planes.

Draftsmen make detailed drawings for a new Boeing plane, the B-1.

In 1919, Boeing (right) and pilot Eddie Hubbard flew the first airmail between Canada and the United States.

Before the B-1 was completed, part of William Boeing's vision of aviation's future was realized. William and a new pilot, Eddie Hubbard, flew a Model C from Seattle, Washington, to Vancouver, British Columbia, Canada. On March 3, 1919, they returned to Seattle with sixty letters. A Boeing plane had carried the first international airmail from Canada to the United States.

24

The Dangers of Early Flight

Early planes had no instruments to guide pilots through fog and storms. On the 125-mile (201-km)-long flight to pick up the international airmail, William and Eddie flew into a storm. Blinding snow blew into the open cockpits. Eddie descended and flew just above the water. He followed the blurred shoreline until he found a safe harbor where he and William stayed for the night.

When the B-1 was completed, Eddie Hubbard flew it for the first time. The plane lifted off the water smoothly, and began to climb. Then the engine sputtered. The fuel pump had failed. Without power the plane's nose pointed up, and like the first

A B-1, with its plywood body, flew passengers and mail from the waters of Washington and British Columbia, Canada.

Model C, the tail was not right. Eddie struggled to keep the plane steady. Pushing the controls as hard as he could, he finally brought the B-1 back to the water.

The fuel pump could be fixed, but the tail had to be redesigned. Early plane building was partly a matter of trial and error.

The design problem was corrected, and Eddie later bought a B-1. He left the company to fly mail between Canada and the United States. However, few other flying boats were sold as William had hoped.

26

Without buyers for new planes, the company would fail. William thought about closing his airplane business. That would mean giving up on his vision for aviation's future. He also felt loyal to his employees, especially Claire Egtvedt and Phil Johnson. So William began to pay his employees from his personal bank account.

Then, in late 1919, the company received an order to rebuild fifty World War I planes. The next year the company built planes designed by the U.S. Army.

Building planes such as this one, but designed by others, kept the company in business during the early 1920s.

In 1921, the army wanted to order two hundred fighter planes. The company that could build the planes at the lowest cost would get the job. William believed his company could build the planes without losing money.

These fighter planes had been designed by another company, but Claire Egtvedt knew the Boeing Airplane Company could design and build a better one. He had watched planes practice aerial combat. He knew the plane that flew the fastest and made the sharpest turns would win.

Claire presented his design ideas to William. Instead of wood, their fighter plane's body would be framed with metal using an electric welding system developed by the company. William listened to Claire, then said, "That's exactly what we should do. Develop the best fighter that can be built."

The next few years brought good and bad times for the company. The two hundred fighter planes for the army were built at a profit, but the company's own fighter plane was not immediately successful. A Boeing trainer plane was accepted by the navy.

The PW-9 was the first military fighter plane designed and built by the Boeing Airplane Company.

Before this plane was perfected, however, there were several crashes. The pilots suffered only minor injuries. Designing planes continued to be a matter of trial and error.

Many leftover World War I planes were still available to buy. Claire Egtvedt talked to barnstorming pilots. They said a World War I plane cost $700, while a new one cost $4,000. One pilot told Claire, "You figure out how many rides I'd have to sell at five dollars each to buy one of your planes."

In 1924, the U.S. Post Office's old military planes were beginning to wear out, and it ordered one new Boeing plane to fly the mail. The two-wing, single-engine, Model 40 rolled out of a Boeing Airplane plant a year later.

The Barnstormers

Barnstorming pilots helped show Americans what planes could do. They flew low over small towns to attract attention, then landed in near-by cow pastures. People stood in line to pay for a short, but thrilling, plane ride of loops and rolls.

In this 1925 photograph, a barnstormer flies the plane while a stuntman works his way down a cable to "ride" a bicycle 3,000 feet (914 m) above the ground.

Chapter FIVE

A Vision Comes True

By 1926, the hard work of William Boeing and his employees had kept the Boeing Airplane Company in business. Their fighter plane, improved in design, had broken speed records and was being flown by both the army and the navy. The welded steel frames pioneered by the company were in common use. Powerful air-cooled engines were replacing water-cooled engines of the past. The company had five hundred employees.

William Boeing still wanted to expand aviation for public use. One day, William's wife Bertha saw an interesting newspaper article. It reported that the U.S. Post Office wanted private companies to fly the airmail routes. She folded the paper so William would see the article. He read it without commenting.

Claire Egtvedt and pilot Eddie Hubbard, who had rejoined the company, were also aware of the opportunity. They wanted to bid on the mail route between Chicago, Illinois, and San Francisco, California. They considered the risks. Planes would be flying at night. Pilots would have only a compass,

Boeing's wife Bertha (left) sometimes visited the plant with her husband (in long coat).

an altitude gauge, and government beacon lights placed every 25 miles (40 km) along the route to guide them.

Claire and Eddie thought the company's Model 40 could be improved to carry 1,000 pounds (454 kilograms) of mail and two passengers. They carefully figured the costs and showed them to William. Finally, he said, "The figures look all right to me, let's send them in."

On January 28, 1927, the company learned it was the lowest bidder. Their costs were far below those presented by others. Some people thought that such low costs would bankrupt the company. But William was confident they could build the planes. Phil

The Model 40 had to fly over mountains to carry mail between Chicago and San Francisco.

Johnson took charge of the new air transport business and work began on twenty-five planes.

For the first time, the Boeing Airplane Company was building a fleet of planes for public use instead of military use. At last, William Boeing's vision was coming true.

Jane Eads thanks her pilot after becoming the first passenger on Boeing's Chicago-to-San Francisco route.

In Chicago on July 1, 1927, a Boeing pilot sat in the open cockpit of a new Model 40-A. He gunned the engine and took off. He headed for San Francisco flying at 135 miles (217 km) per hour. Jane Eads, a Chicago newspaper reporter, sat in a small, enclosed cabin between the wings.

Boeing's air transport business made money in the first six months. It carried 525 passengers

A Pioneering Passenger

Jane Eads was the first woman to fly long distance on a Boeing plane. She watched cities and towns pass below. She felt jolts as the plane landed every few hours for fuel, to change pilots, and sometimes to change planes. She was tossed about in bumpy air and heard the engine surge as the plane climbed above the Rocky Mountains. She was thrilled when they landed in San Francisco.

and 230,000 pounds (104,000 kg) of mail. This success led the company to build larger, three-engine transports that could carry eighteen passengers. Two pilots sat in an enclosed cockpit and received weather reports by two-way radio, a system that was pioneered by the Boeing Airplane Company.

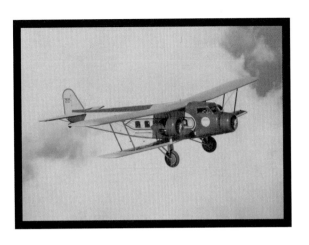

The Model 80 was the first Boeing plane to have an enclosed cockpit for pilots.

Still, William Boeing continued to look ahead. He told a reporter, "We are pioneers in a new science and industry." He also said that the company must, "let no new improvements in flying equipment and flying pass us by."

William Boeing's desire for improvement led to a new era in flight. On May 22, 1930, the Monomail plane flew from Seattle's Boeing Field. It was a single-engine plane made entirely of metal. It had a streamlined body, and its wheels could be retracted (pulled back into the plane's wing) during

The sleek Monomail was a major advance in the design of airplanes.

The Boeing 247 was the first streamlined, all-metal transport plane built in the United States.

flight. Most importantly its wing was braced from the inside. Struts and wires were no longer needed to support the weight of a plane's wing.

The company's engineers next found a way to mount engines on the plane's wing. Then, they designed a twin-engine, single-wing passenger plane, called the Boeing 247.

In February 1933, the 247 took to the skies. It carried ten passengers, cargo, and mail, and traveled 189 miles (304 km) per hour. Including stops for fuel, it could fly from Chicago to San Francisco in less than seventeen hours.

The next year, William Boeing was awarded the Daniel Guggenheim Medal for "successful pioneering and achievement in aircraft manufacturing and air transport."

The Daniel Guggenheim Medal

The Daniel Guggenheim Medal is awarded each year to people who have made important advances in aviation. The medal was first awarded in 1929 when Orville and Wilbur Wright received it.

Chapter SIX

New Horizons

The Boeing Clipper was one of the Boeing Company's flying boats.

William Boeing retired in 1934. He wanted to spend time with his wife and young son, William Jr., and to cruise and fish in northwest waters from his yacht.

A few years after Boeing's retirement, his company's flying boats were carrying passengers across oceans. In the 1940s, more than 16,000 Boeing B-17 and B-29 bombers helped win World War II. Then the company entered the jet age with B-47 air force bombers.

A Boeing B-47 air force bomber

In 1954, William Boeing was the guest of honor when the company's first passenger jet, the Boeing 707, rolled from the hangar. The plane could carry 181 passengers at 600 miles (966 km) per hour. It was far different from the *B & W* William had flown only thirty-eight years before.

William Boeing died on his yacht on September 28, 1956. But, the company he founded continued into the "splendid future" he had foreseen.

Boeing in the cockpit of the United States's first jet passenger plane, the Boeing 707

In this 1954 photograph, admirers inspect the Boeing 707.

The Boeing 747 is the largest passenger plane ever built. A Boeing Lunar Rover carried American astronauts on the surface of the moon. The president of the United States flies in a Boeing 747 called *Air Force One.* And, every day, people throughout the world board Boeing planes to fly to distant places.

A Boeing 747 is large enough to carry a United States space shuttle on its back.

**Boeing Lunar Rovers carried U.S. astronauts across
the surface of the Moon. In this 1972 photograph,
astronaut Gene Cernan drives the rover.**

In Your Community

Today, we all enjoy the results of William Boeing's vision. He wanted to build planes so people, packages, and mail could travel fast and far.

Planes are also used to search for lost people, to drop water on forest fires, and to report automobile traffic for radio stations. Can you think of other ways that planes are used?

Is there an airport near your community? Is it for small planes or jet planes? It is fun to visit an airport

Timeline

1881 — William E. Boeing is born on October 1 in Detroit, Michigan.

1900 — William enters Yale University to study engineering.

1903 — William moves to Washington State; the Wright Brothers fly the world's first plane.

1914 — William takes his first plane ride; World War I begins.

1916 — William flies the *B & W*; starts his airplane company.

1917 — The United States enters World War I; the Boeing Airplane Company builds military planes.

1918 — World War I ends.

and, no matter what size the planes, it is exciting to watch them take off and land. Some airports have tours. You can take a tour with an adult and learn about airports.

Would you like to make a model airplane? Libraries have books that show how to build them, and hobby shops have model airplane kits.

Maybe your vision of the future is about planes. You could become an aircraft engineer or you could even learn to fly and become a pilot.

| 1919 | 1921 | 1927 | 1933 | 1934 | 1954 | 1956 |

William and Eddie Hubbard carry the first airmail between Canada and the United States.

Boeing Airplane Company planes begin to fly airmail and passengers between Chicago and San Francisco.

Boeing receives the Daniel Guggenheim Medal.

William Boeing dies on September 28 at the age of seventy-four.

William marries Bertha Paschall; Boeing's company begins to build fighter planes for the army.

The Boeing Monomail is flown.

The Boeing Company's first passenger jet is completed.

To Find Out More

Here are some additional resources to help you learn more about William Boeing, planes, and flying adventures:

Books

Barrett, Norman. *Flying Machines.* Franklin Watts, 1994.

Jefferies, David. *Flight: Fliers and Flying Machines.* Franklin Watts, 1997.

Mansfield, Harold. *Vision: A Saga of the Sky, The Original Story of Boeing.* Madison Publishing Associates, 1986.

Taylor, Richard L. *The First Flight: The Story of the Wright Brothers.* Franklin Watts, 1990.

Taylor, Richard L. *The First Solo Flight Around the World.* Franklin Watts, 1993.

Online Sites

Museum of Flight
9404 E. Marginal Way South
Seattle, Washington 98108
http://www.museumofflight.org
Here you can see the "Red Barn," the birthplace of The Boeing Company, dozens of full-size aircraft, and much more!

National Air and Space Museum
Smithsonian Institution
Independence Avenue
    at 6th Street, SW
Washington, D.C. 20560
http://www.nasm.si.edu
Among the hundreds of exhibits on display, you can see the plane the Wright Brothers flew at Kitty Hawk, a lunar module, and a space shuttle cockpit simulator.

Western Museum of Flight
12016 Prairie Avenue
Hawthorne, California 90250
http://www.wmof.com
This museum's collection features many different kinds of aircraft, flight simulators, engines, aviation instruments, and more.

Index

About the Authors

Sharlene and Ted Nelson live near Seattle, Washington, on a hill overlooking the waters of Puget Sound. They have written books about lighthouses, national parks, logging in the Old West, and sailing on the Columbia River.

From their home, the Nelsons can see and hear Boeing jets take off from the Seattle-Tacoma International Airport. Some jets turn west to fly to places such as Hawaii and Japan. Others turn east to fly to Chicago, Atlanta, New York, or other cities. From their windows, the Nelsons see small planes with pontoons skim over the water and land nearby.

Many times they have visited Seattle's Museum of Flight, which includes the Boeing Airplane Company's original "Red Barn." At the museum, they have enjoyed watching people restoring historic planes.